MAR - 6 2018

STEM *trailblazer* BIOS

GENIUS
PHYSICIST
ALBERT EINSTEIN

KATIE MARSICO

Lerner Publications ◆ Minneapolis

To my friends in PAGE, who—like Einstein—are all talented, intelligent, and unafraid to ask questions

Content consultant: Liliya L. R. Williams, professor at the Minnesota Institute for Astrophysics

Copyright © 2018 by Lerner Publishing Group, Inc.

All rights reserved. International copyright secured. No part of this book may be reproduced, stored in a retrieval system, or transmitted in any form or by any means—electronic, mechanical, photocopying, recording, or otherwise—without the prior written permission of Lerner Publishing Group, Inc., except for the inclusion of brief quotations in an acknowledged review.

Lerner Publications Company
A division of Lerner Publishing Group, Inc.
241 First Avenue North
Minneapolis, MN 55401 USA

For reading levels and more information, look up this title at www.lernerbooks.com.

Library of Congress Cataloging-in-Publication Data

Names: Marsico, Katie, 1980–
Title: Genius physicist Albert Einstein / Katie Marsico.
Description: Minneapolis : Lerner Publications, ©2018. | Series: STEM trailblazer bios | Audience: Age 7–11. | Audience: Grade 4 to 6. | Includes bibliographical references and index.
Identifiers: LCCN 2016056356 (print) | LCCN 2017006205 (ebook) | ISBN 9781512434514 (lb : alk. paper) | ISBN 9781512456295 (pb : alk. paper) | ISBN 9781512451030 (eb pdf)
Subjects: LCSH: Einstein, Albert, 1879–1955—Juvenile literature. | Physicists—Biography—Juvenile literature.
Classification: LCC QC16.E5 M3295 2018 (print) | LCC QC16.E5 (ebook) | DDC 530.092 [B]—dc23
LC record available at https://lccn.loc.gov/2016056356

Manufactured in the United States of America
1-42100-25394-3/1/2017

The images in this book are used with the permission of: © Bridgeman Images, p. 4; Keystone Pictures USA/Alamy Stock Photo, pp. 5, 26; Wikimedia Commons, pp. 6, 14; ETH-Bibliothek Zürich, Bildarchiv/Wikimedia Commons, p. 9; Pictorial Press Ltd/Alamy Stock Photo, p. 10; age fotostock/Alamy Stock Photo, p. 11; Library of Congress (LC-DIG-ppmsc-06808), p. 12; © ullstein bild/Getty Images, p. 16; © Laura Westlund/Independent Picture Service, p. 19; ESA–C.Carreau, p. 20; Library of Congress (LC-DIG-hec-31012), p. 21; Library of Congress (LC-DIG-hec-31011), p. 22; NASA/SDO, p. 23; Benjamin Couprie, Institut International de Physique de Solvay/Wikimedia Commons, p. 24; Pictures From History/Newscom, p. 28.

Front cover: Library of Congress (LC-USZ62-60242).

Main body text set in Adrianna Regular 13/22. Typeface provided by Chank.

CONTENTS

Albert Einstein was fourteen years old when he posed for this photo in Munich, Germany.

THE BOY FEW PEOPLE BELIEVED IN

Albert Einstein was a famous mathematician and **physicist**. He used his imagination to form incredible ideas about time, space, and **matter**. But most of the people he knew weren't impressed by young Albert. A teacher even told him that he would never amount to much.

Albert proved everyone wrong. His ideas made him famous—ideas that forever changed the way people viewed the universe around them.

FROM CLASSROOM TO CLERK'S OFFICE

Albert Einstein was born on March 14, 1879, in Ulm, Germany. Soon the Einsteins moved to Munich, Germany, to set up the family business. Albert's father was an engineer and salesman of equipment used to produce electricity.

Albert's father, Hermann, and mother, Pauline, knew their son was different from other children.

Albert poses with his younger sister, Maja.

Albert's family suspected he was highly intelligent, though not everyone at school realized it. His family trusted him to walk around the neighborhood on his own before he was four years old. His sister once watched him build a house out of playing cards. He kept at it until the house was an incredible fourteen stories tall. He learned to focus his mind, a skill that would someday help him imagine the universe in unique ways.

Albert was fascinated by how the world around him worked. When he was five years old, his father gave him a compass. Albert was amazed at the way magnetism made the compass needle move.

In 1896, Einstein started attending college in Switzerland. He studied math and physics and graduated in 1900. In 1902, he accepted a position as a patent clerk in Bern, Switzerland. A patent is a license issued by the government. The owner of a patent is the only one with the right to produce or sell a particular invention. Einstein examined invention ideas that people brought to the patent office. In his spare time, he thought about his own unique ideas involving science.

TECH TALK

"The true sign of intelligence is not knowledge but imagination."

—Albert Einstein

STILL FOCUSED ON PHYSICS

In 1903, Einstein married Mileva Maric. A year later, she gave birth to their first son, Hans Albert. Einstein worked at the patent office six days a week to support his family. When he wasn't there, he often spent time discussing physics with his friends.

Even when he was alone, Einstein couldn't stop thinking about physics. Though he had studied the subject in college, much of what he knew he had taught himself. But he still had many questions about popular physics **theories**.

Einstein conducted thought experiments. These were scientific tests that he carried out in his mind. Einstein used his brilliant imagination to understand physics in entirely new ways. He devised theories that asked people to reimagine the boundaries of motion, time, and space.

Einstein said some of his best ideas were hatched at the patent office.

Chapter 2

Einstein wanted to know how different physics theories fit together.

SOLVING A MYSTERY OF MOTION

In the summer of 1905, Einstein published his special theory of relativity. He created this theory to solve a mystery of motion. The mystery involved the work of two other physicists—Isaac Newton (1643–1727) and James Clerk Maxwell (1831–1879).

Newton's theories were shaped by the idea that motion is relative—in other words, the way an object moves depends upon the movement of the person observing it.

For example, passengers on a train may not feel as if they're moving at all. This is because, relative to the train, they're sitting still. But to people watching the train zoom past, it seems as if the passengers are racing along! Relative to people standing on the ground, the train—and everyone in it—are moving extremely fast.

To Einstein, sometimes relative motion made perfect sense. Yet it didn't when he thought about Maxwell's work. He believed that within a **vacuum**, the speed of light never changes. It doesn't move any faster or slower, no matter who is observing it.

James Clerk Maxwell made many exciting discoveries, including the idea that Saturn's rings are made of many small pieces of matter.

FROM THOUGHT EXPERIMENT TO THEORY

Who was right—Newton or Maxwell? To set the scene for his thought experiment, Einstein turned to his real-life experiences in Bern. Einstein sometimes traveled through the city in a streetcar. While riding, he often caught sight of Bern's clock tower.

Einstein pictured his streetcar moving at the speed of light. That's pretty fast— about 186,000 miles (300,000 kilometers) per second! Einstein imagined staring at the clock tower as he sped along. He also studied his watch. How did both clocks look?

Einstein was moving away from the clock tower at the same speed

Einstein often passed Bern's clock tower while traveling in city streetcars.

that light from the tower traveled. So that clock appeared to have stopped. How about his watch? No matter how fast the streetcar he was riding in moved, his watch kept ticking normally.

Suddenly Einstein realized he had solved the mystery! Maxwell was right—the speed of light is constant. Yet Newton was also correct—motion is relative. Einstein decided two people can have different observations of the exact same beam of light. Each person sees the beam differently because each one experiences time differently. So time itself is relative to a person's speed and location.

In his special theory of relativity, Einstein stated that the laws of physics never change. For two objects moving at constant speeds, motion is relative. The theory also describes how the speed of light is constant. This is always true, no matter who observes the light.

MAKING SENSE OF MASS AND ENERGY

In September 1905, Einstein published another theory. It was an entirely new way of understanding mass and energy. Mass is the amount of matter in an object. Energy is the ability to do work.

Until 1905, most scientists viewed mass and energy as separate. Unlike energy, mass was something people could touch and see. A person could examine an object and measure how much of it there was. Scientists found it harder to observe energy. Still, they knew that energy is neither created nor destroyed. Instead, it simply changes form.

Yet Einstein believed that mass and energy aren't separate at all. His theory stated that mass is simply another form of energy. So mass can be changed into energy, and energy can

The United Nations declared 2005 an International Year of Physics to celebrate the one hundredth anniversary of Einstein's greatest discoveries.

be changed into mass. Einstein used what he knew about relativity and the speed of light to show how this happens. His **equation**, $E = mc^2$, is among the most famous equations in science. Einstein explained that E = energy, m = an object's mass, and c^2 = light's constant speed multiplied by itself.

Einstein's miracle year, as scientists later called it, stirred up many different reactions. Some people were in disbelief. After all, Einstein had turned widely accepted physics theories upside down. In the next century, scientists relied upon Einstein's ideas to unfold countless scientific wonders. These ranged from new forms of energy to technology used in space exploration!

Chapter 3

Einstein's discoveries made him one of the world's most famous scientists.

RETHINKING RELATIVITY

Einstein's fame grew after his miracle year. His curiosity and imagination reminded people that they still had much to learn about the universe. Einstein's unique way of thinking led to new job opportunities for him.

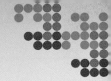

TECH TALK

"I have no special talents. I am only passionately curious."

—Albert Einstein

Between 1911 and 1914, Einstein worked as a college professor in Czechoslovakia, Switzerland, and Germany. By then, Einstein had another son. Eduard was born in 1910.

Einstein continued his thought experiments. He worked day and night to understand how different physics ideas fit together. How did his special theory of relativity make sense alongside what people knew about gravity?

Newton said gravity is the force that attracts objects to one another. It's why objects naturally move toward the ground. According to Newton, gravity exists across the universe. It controls the movement of the sun, moon, planets, and stars.

Newton described how mass and distance affect gravitational force. Objects with more mass experience more gravitational pull. Objects that are farther apart experience less gravitational pull.

With Newton's ideas in mind, Einstein thought about special relativity. The problem with relativity was that it only covered objects experiencing inertia. These objects travel in a straight line and at a constant speed.

In real life, however, outside forces—such as gravity—affect motion all the time. Gravity causes objects to travel along curved paths and accelerate, or speed up. Einstein knew he had to make his theory fit these situations too.

FAR MORE THAN A FORCE

Einstein turned to another thought experiment. He pictured himself riding in an elevator. What would happen if the cable supporting the elevator snapped? Einstein knew the elevator would fall.

When the cable snapped, Einstein and the elevator accelerated toward the ground. Gravity caused his body and the elevator to fall in the same direction at the same speed. This made Einstein feel weightless—almost as if he were floating! Since the elevator had no windows, he couldn't see how he was moving in relation to anything outside the elevator. And he didn't know if it was gravity or some other force that was causing his motion.

Einstein published his general theory of relativity in 1915. It stated that from a moving object, an observer can't tell the difference between gravity and acceleration. The effect of these forces is relative. According to Einstein, gravity is far more than a force. It is a curve in time and space.

IMAGINING AN INCREDIBLE CURVE

To better understand general relativity, people often imagine three objects: a bowling ball, a marble, and a trampoline. A trampoline has a flat surface. But if someone sets a bowling ball on it, the trampoline's surface curves. If someone puts a marble on the trampoline, the marble rolls along the curve.

The more mass an object has, the more it bends space and time.

In this example, the trampoline is time and space. The bowling ball represents a large object such as a star or planet. The marble is an object with less mass—maybe a moon or an asteroid. Mass causes time and space to curve. Einstein said that gravity is how different objects react to this curve.

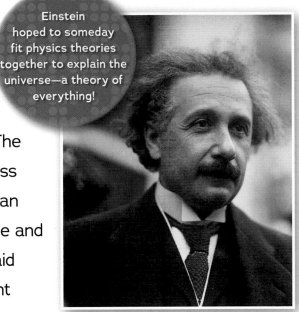

Einstein hoped to someday fit physics theories together to explain the universe—a theory of everything!

Some scientists found it hard to accept Einstein's vision. Other people were excited by it. They believed the theory would be the start of even more exciting scientific breakthroughs. Later, Einstein's supporters would be proven right.

The idea of general relativity plays an important part in the modern **Global Positioning System (GPS)**. GPS devices rely on satellites with special clocks. Thanks to Einstein, scientists know that the movement of satellites in orbit is relative to Earth's movement. This helps scientists adjust GPS equipment to make it accurate. People have even discussed using Einstein's theory to unlock the mystery of time travel. Scientists can't do it yet, but they haven't given up!

Chapter 4

Einstein and Elsa Löwenthal traveled to Washington, DC, together.

CHALLENGES AND TRIUMPHS

Einstein's general theory of relativity made him even more famous. Yet he paid a price for his fame and tireless work. In 1917, Einstein was exhausted and became seriously ill. By then, he and Mileva were divorced. Elsa Löwenthal cared for him. Einstein and Löwenthal married in 1919.

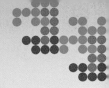

For Einstein, 1919 was an important year for other reasons as well. It was when he finally proved his general theory of relativity. Until then, Einstein's thought experiments had impressed people. But ideas were not the same as evidence.

That year, scientists watched the sky as they awaited a solar eclipse. During an eclipse, the moon passes between the sun and Earth. For a brief time, the moon blocks the sun's light.

According to Einstein, the eclipse was an opportunity to observe general relativity in action. If his ideas were correct, the sun's gravity would cause starlight to bend. It would look as though the stars had taken new positions in the sky. When the eclipse occurred, this is exactly what happened. Einstein was proven right!

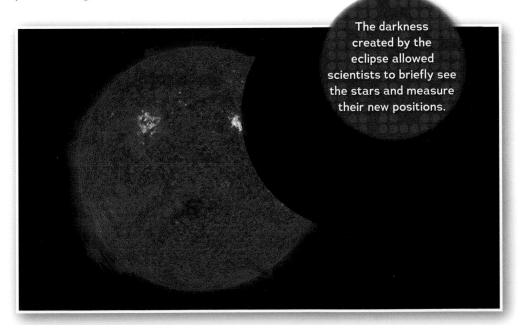

The darkness created by the eclipse allowed scientists to briefly see the stars and measure their new positions.

RECOGNITION AND RESEARCH

In 1922, Einstein received the Nobel Prize in Physics. A growing number of people viewed him as a genius. Einstein continued teaching and doing research.

During the late 1920s, Einstein studied quantum mechanics with Danish physicist Niels Bohr. This branch of physics focuses on the tiniest units, or particles, of matter that exist within each **atom**. Einstein and Bohr explored the way these particles move. They tried to use math to describe their motion.

Einstein *(front row center)* was seen as a genius by both the public and his fellow physicists.

TECH TALK

"The only way to escape the . . . effect of praise is to go on working."

—*Albert Einstein*

SETTLING IN THE UNITED STATES

In December 1932, Einstein visited Pasadena, California, with his wife, Elsa. He did research at the California Institute of Technology. The Einsteins planned to head back to Germany in March 1933. Then they heard news that changed their minds.

In early 1933, Adolf Hitler of the Nazi Party became the leader of Germany. The Nazis were **prejudiced** against many groups, including Jews. Since Einstein was Jewish, he chose not to return home. The Einsteins settled in Princeton, New Jersey. Einstein accepted a job at a research center there.

Elsa Einstein died just three years later. Einstein was heartbroken but continued to work as hard as ever. Meanwhile, he prepared to celebrate another important achievement. In 1940, he became a US citizen.

chapter 5

Einstein's mind never rested. He's shown here calculating the mass of the Milky Way galaxy.

TIMELESS TALENT AND INTELLIGENCE

In 1941, the United States entered World War II (1939–1945). Einstein urged the US government to research nuclear power. That's the energy released when an atom's center splits. Einstein knew nuclear power could fuel highly destructive bombs.

He believed it had to be used responsibly. After the war, Einstein worked with other scientists to ensure that it would be.

INSPIRING FURTHER EXPLORATION

On April 18, 1955, Einstein died of heart failure. His life was over, but his story and achievements have remained timeless. For Einstein, physics didn't just involve laws and equations. His creativity and imagination allowed him to see the world in ways that few others could have imagined.

PROMOTING WORLD PEACE

In 1945, US and Japanese forces were battling each other in World War II. Then the United States dropped an atomic bomb on the Japanese cities of Hiroshima and Nagasaki. More than 150,000 people died instantly. Not long afterward, Japan surrendered.

Einstein hadn't been directly involved in US efforts to create the bombs. Yet he was troubled by what had occurred in Japan. He worked with scientists and world leaders to prevent another nuclear attack.

More than sixty years after his death, Einstein is still one of the world's most famous physicists.

Modern scientists still turn to Einstein's theories to solve mysteries. They use his work to examine ideas that don't always seem possible. Einstein's life inspires people to keep exploring the vast universe around them.

TIMELINE

1879

Albert Einstein is born in Ulm, Germany, on March 14.

1902

Einstein accepts a job as a patent clerk in Bern, Switzerland.

1905

During what people eventually call his miracle year, Einstein publishes several groundbreaking theories, including his special theory of relativity and an equation that shows how mass can be changed into energy (and vice versa).

1915

Einstein publishes his general theory of relativity.

1919

Einstein's general theory of relativity is proven correct during a solar eclipse.

1922

Einstein receives the Nobel Prize in Physics.

1932

Einstein visits Pasadena, California, in December with his wife, Elsa.

1933

The Einsteins settle in Princeton, New Jersey, after Adolf Hitler's rise to power in Germany.

1945

The United States drops two atomic bombs on Japan. Einstein begins work to promote peace and prevent further nuclear warfare.

1955

On April 18, Einstein dies of heart failure at a hospital in Princeton, New Jersey.

SOURCE NOTES

7   Albert Einstein, quoted in Max Miller, "What Is Intelligence?," *Big Think*, accessed January 12, 2017, http://bigthink.com/going-mental/what-is -intelligence-2.

17 Albert Einstein, quoted in Gretchen Rubin, "I Have No Special Talents, I Am Only Passionately Curious," *Psychology Today*, March 7, 2011, https://www .psychologytoday.com/blog/the-happiness-project/201103/i-have-no-special -talents-i-am-only-passionately-curious.

25 Albert Einstein, quoted in Benna and Baer, "25 Quotes."

GLOSSARY

atom
the smallest piece of an element

equation
a math or science statement that shows how two things are equal

Global Positioning System (GPS)
technology that uses satellites to help people navigate

matter
the substance that makes up any physical object

physicist
a scientist who specializes in the study of matter and energy

prejudiced
passing unfair judgment against a person or group (often based on race or religion)

theories
unproven ideas that provide possible explanations for facts or events

vacuum
a space that is entirely empty of matter

FURTHER INFORMATION

BOOKS

Anderson, Jennifer Joline. *Albert Einstein: Revolutionary Physicist.* Minneapolis: Core Library, 2015. Read more about Einstein's life and accomplishments.

Cornell, Kari. *Theoretical Physicist Stephen Hawking.* Minneapolis: Lerner Publications, 2016. Do you want to know the secrets of the universe? Learn about a physicist who is looking for answers.

Romero, Libby. *Albert Einstein.* Washington, DC: National Geographic, 2016. What other ideas did Einstein use to reshape physics? Read more about this famous scientist and his achievements.

WEBSITES

Albert Einstein in the World Wide Web—Biography
http://www.einstein-website.de/z_kids/biographykids.html
Check out more fascinating details of Einstein's amazing life and achievements.

Ducksters—Theory of Relativity
http://www.ducksters.com/science/physics/theory_of_relativity.php
Check out this site for further explanation of Einstein's ideas about relativity.

Science Kids—Albert Einstein Facts
http://www.sciencekids.co.nz/sciencefacts/scientists/alberteinstein.html
Visit this site for Einstein quotes, as well as fast facts about his life and theories.

Expand learning beyond the printed book. Download free, complementary educational resources for this book from our website, www.lerneresource.com.

INDEX

ABOUT THE AUTHOR

Katie Marsico has written more than two hundred books for kids
and young adults. She lives near Chicago, Illinois, with her husband
and six children. Marsico graduated from the Medill School of
Journalism at Northwestern University. Before becoming an author,
she worked as an editor of children's reference books.